Happy Within

By Marisa J. Taylor

Illustrated by Vanessa Balleza

I love the color of my skin. I am unique and beautiful within.

I take pride in who I am and what I can do.

Being me makes me happy from within.

I love to sing, dance and play with my friends, but that is just me, that makes me happy.

What about you?

What makes you happy?

Some of my friends love to play with toys and make a lot of noise.

That is okay too, because to them it brings joy.

Some of my friends love to sing, dance and chat away. That's okay, because everyone is different and special in their own way.

I do my best to be the best version of me.

I do not compare myself to the other children I see. I am proud of who I am and free to be me.

Some children will say things and make you feel sad.

Don´t pay attention to their words and continue to be glad.

Let's support one another to be the best we can be.

Everyone is unique in their own special way.

Be happy with who you are and what you see.

It doesn't matter where in the world you are from, nor the color of your skin.

BE YOU and do what makes you happy from within.

The moment you feel the
butterflies inside and have a
smile on your face, do more
of that to make you grin.

One thing to remember
in order to be happy
from within...

Look at yourself in the mirror and say out loud
"I am the best version of me and happy within my skin."

If you believe in and love yourself,
you can achieve anything and win.

BEING ME MAKES ME

· ·

WHAT ABOUT YOU?
WHAT MAKES YOU HAPPY?

Happy Within
Copyright © Lingo Babies, 2020

Written by Marisa J. Taylor
Illustrations: Vanessa Balleza

ISBN: 978-1-9163956-7-1
Graphic Design: Clementina Cortés

CPSIA information can be obtained
at www.ICGtesting.com
Printed in the USA
LVHW070933240522
719564LV00006BA/13